Connie the Conjunction

Written by Coert Voorhees
Illustrations by Powerhouse Animation

Meet the Parts of Speech

I name a specific person, place, thing, or idea. It's a big responsibility, naming things—a responsibility that requires a certain attention to detail.

Vinny the Action Verb

Some people say I'm all over the place. Some people call me a ball of energy. I take that as a compliment, because I just like to go, go, go!

I take the place of one or more Nouns or Pronouns. I always want the Noun's job, and I hang out with the Verb and Adjective.

Lucy the Linking Verb

I'm perfectly happy to link Nouns and Pronouns with the appropriate Adjectives, but it's not like I'm going to expend a lot of energy doing so.

I modify a Noun or Pronoun. I tell what kind, which one, how many, or how much. I pride myself on being the most artistic of the parts of speech.

Connie the Conjunction

Gather 'round everybody and let's have ourselves a wonderful time. I just love bringing words and groups of words together, don't you?

I modify a Verb, Adjective, or other Adverb. I tell how, when, where, to what extent, and under what condition. I often end in –ly, but I don't have to.

Izzy the Interjection

I express emotion!! Yep, I'm always here, always ready with my commas and exclamation points, just in case.

They call me Preposition because I'm pre-positioned. I'm first. At the front. Before every other word in the phrase? Got it?

Slang

I am a chameleon. A spy. An undercover operative. I infiltrate the sentence and act as whatever part of speech suits me.

CONNIE THE CONJUNCTION

Graphic Design by Mckee Frazior

This book is typeset in Komika Text

Distributed throughout the world by Ingram Publisher Services www.ingrambook.com

Connie the conjunction joined words, phrases, and clauses.
Come on in and shop until you drop!
Connie's Couture

She had the best sense of style in all of Grammaropolis because she knew how to put things together.
Are we going for common or proper?

Everyone trusted Connie's taste.

If her customers ever fought over an item, she made sure they got along.
Boys, boys!
That's my shirt!
No, it's mine!

Connie used her conjunctions to solve the problem.
I have one for Roger and one for Jake!

She loved all the conjunctions, but her favorites were the coordinating conjunctions. She called them "FANBOYS" for short.

Connie could use one of the FANBOYS to link two words.
Great choice. The jacket and tie are perfect together.
and

She could use one of the FANBOYS to link two phrases.
I recommend choosing the striped shirt or the polka-dot pants.
or
Coordinating Conjunctions
for and nor but or yet so

Connie could even use one of the FANBOYS to link two independent clauses.

One day, Jake was so proud of his new outfit that he forgot to mop the wet floor.

Connie felt a little dizzy, but she jumped up and got right back to work.
Lucy, I've changed my mind. Take the skirt and those boots and that jacket.

Unfortunately, she was still a bit dazed, and her sense of style was completely mixed up.
You're a big superhero, yet you never wear cow-covered tights.
V

You will not regret this, nor will you be mistaken for a pronoun.

Her dizziness wore off eventually, but the damage had been done.
What happened here?
Whoa, dude. Wardrobe malfunction!

She tried to fix it with the FANBOYS.
Would you rather get rid of the tights or the cape?
Can I choose both?
But coordinating conjunctions weren't strong enough.

She needed something stronger.

First she tried correlative conjunctions. She used them to link words and word groups used in exactly the same way.
Get rid of both the cape and the tights.
both... and
Correlative Conjunctions
either... or
not only... but also
neither... nor

The correlative conjunctions helped, but even they weren't quite strong enough.

She brought out the subordinating conjunctions, which she used to introduce subordinate clauses.
Because your smile is so pretty, you shouldn't hide it with that shirt.
Remove those roller skates so that you don't fall.
Subordinating Conjunctions
even though
so that
before
because
whenever
while

Putting a subordinating conjunction at the beginning of the clause made the clause dependent, which meant that it couldn't stand on its own.
Whenever I see you in those pants, I giggle.
I suggest you go back to your old look even though I like that shirt.

Finally, everything was back in order.
Where are my FANBOYS?
Well, almost everything.

This shirt is bright and handsome and paisley and colorful, so it's not ugly or grey or long-sleeved or...
Coordinating Conjunctions
for and nor but or yet so
Stylin'.

Functions of Conjunctions

A conjunction joins words or word groups. Yes, indeed!

JOINING WORDS

A conjunction can join words.

EXAMPLES

and

or

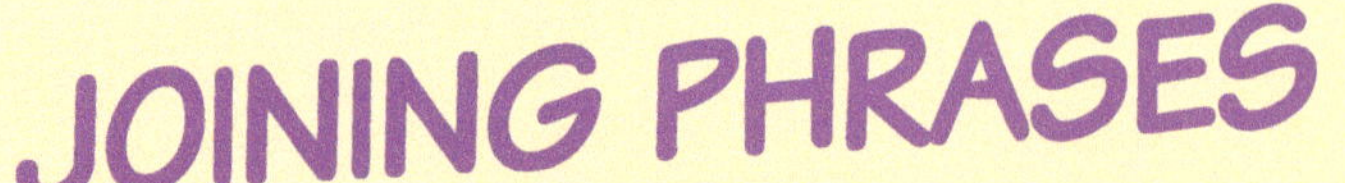

JOINING PHRASES

A conjunction can join phrases.

I keep my treasure under the bed or in a box.

Penguins have white bellies and black wings.

EXAMPLES

and

or

JOINING CLAUSES

A conjunction can join clauses.

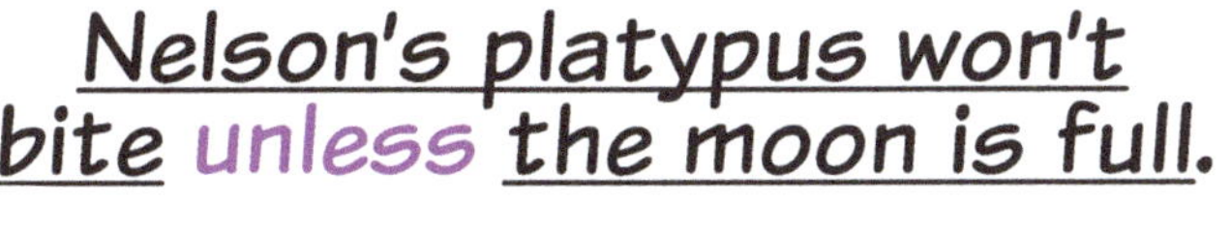

Sarah told me a funny joke, and I laughed for five minutes!

EXAMPLES

unless

and

COORDINATING CONJUNCTIONS

A *coordinating conjunction* is used to join words, phrases, or independent clauses.

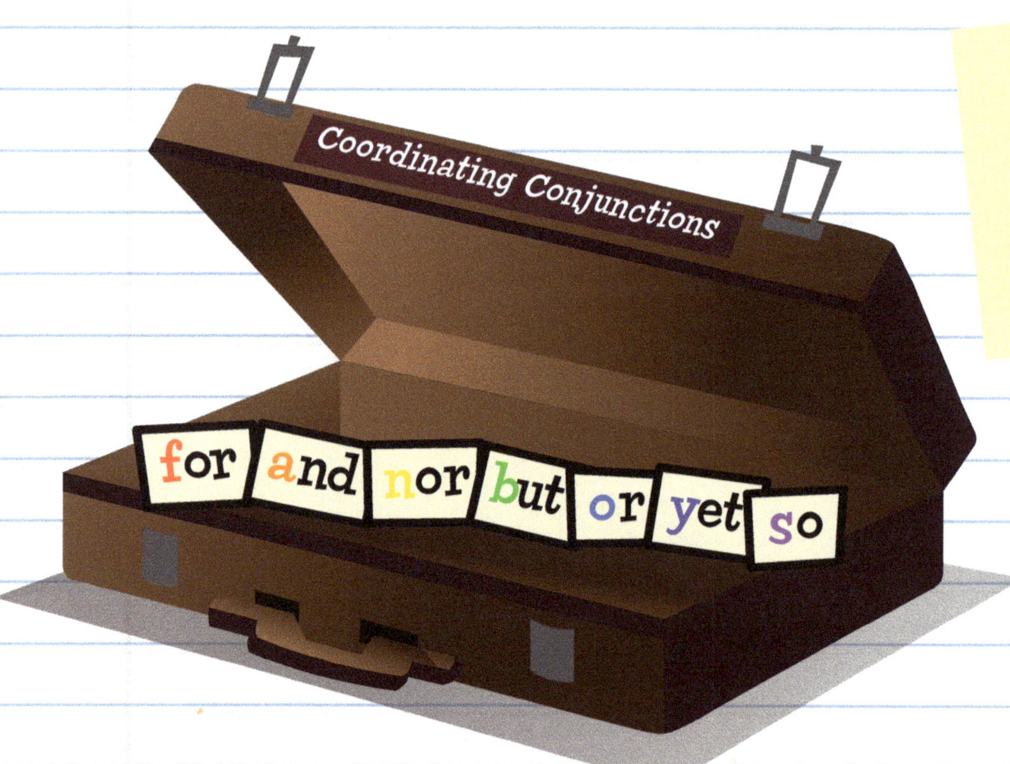

WORDS

Albert's sister just gave me milk and cookies.

PHRASES

Would you prefer to live in the city or in the country?

INDEPENDENT CLAUSES

My grandfather is very old, yet he looks just like me.

FANBOYS:

for, and, nor, but, or, yet, so

SUBORDINATING CONJUNCTIONS

A subordinating conjunction introduces a subordinate (dependent) clause, which is a group of words with a subject and predicate that doesn't make sense on its own.

EXAMPLES

because
Wherever

CORRELATIVE CONJUNCTIONS

A correlative conjunction is a two-part conjunction used to join words or phrases used in the same way.

Both my little sister and my elderly grandmother are fans of the Disney channel.

I am allowed to play either in the front yard or in the back yard.

EXAMPLES

Both...and

either...or

CPSIA information can be obtained
at www.ICGtesting.com
Printed in the USA
BVHW020504110519
547997BV00002B/4/P